Kid's Box

New Generation

Caroline Nixon &
Michael Tomlinson

Student's Book
with eBook

American English

3

Language summary

	Key vocabulary	Key language	Sounds and spelling
Hello! page 4	**Character names:** *Scott, Sally, Suzy* **Numbers:** *1–20* **Colors:** *black, blue, gray, green, orange, pink, purple, red, white, yellow* **Toys:** *bike, camera, computer, doll, game, helicopter, kite, monster, train, truck*	**Introductions:** *Hello. What's your name? My name's … How old are you? I'm … What's her/his name? Her/His name's …* **Present progressive** (not with future reference) **Prepositions of place:** *next to, on, in front of, under, between, behind*	*i–e* – ride *y* – fly *ay* – play *ai* – paint *ei* – eight *a–e* – late
1 Family matters page 10	**Family:** *aunt, uncle, daughter, son, granddaughter, grandson, parents, grandparents* **Appearance:** *beard, curly hair, fair hair, straight hair, mustache, naughty, quiet*	**Possessive 's** **Present progressive for ongoing actions** **Simple present:** *Yes, I do. / No, I don't.* **Verb + infinitive:** *want to do* **Verb + ing:** *like / love / enjoy doing*	*er* – dinner

Math: How big is your family?   page 16

	Key vocabulary	Key language	Sounds and spelling
2 Home sweet home page 18	**Numbers:** *12–100* **The home:** *apartment, balcony, basement, downstairs, elevator, stairs, upstairs* **The world around us:** *city, the country, town*	*What's your address? It's …* **Present progressive for ongoing actions** **Simple present:** *need/needs, have / has*	*ee* – sheep

Geography: How are our homes unique?   page 24

Review: units 1 and 2   page 26

	Key vocabulary	Key language	Sounds and spelling
3 A day in the life page 28	**Daily routines:** *catch the bus, do homework, get dressed, get undressed, get up, go to bed/ school, put on, seven o'clock, take a shower, take off, wake up, wash* **Days of the week:** *Monday, Tuesday, Wednesday, Thursday, Friday, Saturday, Sunday*	**Simple present** (for routines) *How often …? I always …* **Adverbs:** *always, sometimes, never, every day*	/iz/ – dances /z/ – plays /s/ – eats

Science: What do astronauts do in space?   page 34

	Key vocabulary	Key language	Sounds and spelling
4 In the city page 36	**Places:** *bank, bus station, hospital, library, market, movie theater, parking lot, sports center, store, supermarket, swimming pool*	*Where's the …? It's …* **Prepositions of place** **Infinitive of purpose** *Have/Has to for obligation*	*ere* – where *ear* – bear *air* – hair

Geography: Where do we go shopping?   page 42

Review: units 3 and 4   page 44

Hello!

Scott Sally Suzy

 2 **Read and say the name. Listen and check.**

a Hello. I'm nine. I have a brother and a sister. This is my favorite computer game. It's called "Brainbox."

b Hello. I'm five. I have a big dog. She's black and white, and her name's Dotty.

c Hi. I'm eight. I like reading comic books. My favorite comic book's called *Lock and Key*.

2 **Ask and answer. Write.**

What's your name? My name's …

1 What's your name?
2 How old are you?
3 Do you have a brother or a sister?
4 What's your favorite toy called?

My name's Zak. I'm nine.

LOOK

My favorite comic book's **called** *Lock and Key*.

Vocabulary: character names | **Language:** introductions

1 🎧 3 Listen and say the number and the color.

H-E-L-M-E-T

Helmet. That's number 18, and it's pink and green.

2 Play the game.

B-I-K-E

Bike. That's number 17, and it's purple.

3 Read and answer.

Computer.

1 It's on the table, next to the books.
2 It's on the box, next to the ball.
3 It's on the floor, in front of the train.
4 It's under the table.
5 It's on the floor, between the helicopter and the monster.
6 It's behind the bike.

Read and match the names. Eva – c

SCHOOL

Scott and Sally are on the playground with their friends, Alex , Robert , and Eva , and their sister Suzy. Eva's sitting next to Sally, and Scott's talking to Robert. Alex is behind them.

DETECTIVE BOX

 Listen. Who is it?

She's drinking orange juice.   That's Eva.

3 Answer the questions.

1 What's Sally doing?   She's reading.
2 What's Alex doing?
3 What's Robert eating?
4 What's Suzy doing?

5 What's Eva drinking?
6 What's Scott doing?
7 What's Alex kicking?
8 What's Sally reading?

STUDY

What**'s** Suzy doing?   What **is** Suzy doing?
She**'s** jumping.   She **is** jumping.

Language: prepositions of place and present progressive

 **Listen and say the name.**

I have an old bike,
And I'm riding it.
He has a big kite,
And he's flying it.
She has a small car,
And she's driving it.

We have toys!

I have a big doll,
And it's talking.
He has a robot,
And it's walking.
She has a new ball,
And it's bouncing.

We have toys!

 **Listen and sing. Do karaoke.**

 Read and complete.

1 Yasmin's ___holding___ a big doll.
2 Fred's _____ an old bike.
3 Max is _____ a big kite.

4 Vicky's _____ a small car.
5 Anna's _____ a new ball.
6 Paul's _____ with a robot.

Lock's sounds and spelling

1 🎧 7 ▶ **Watch the video. Watch again and practice.**

2 **Find the sounds and draw a circle or a triangle. Say.**

> ○
> The spiders ride, fly, and drive from nine to five.
> △
> They play and paint from eight to late.

3 **Work in pairs. Play, ask, and answer.**

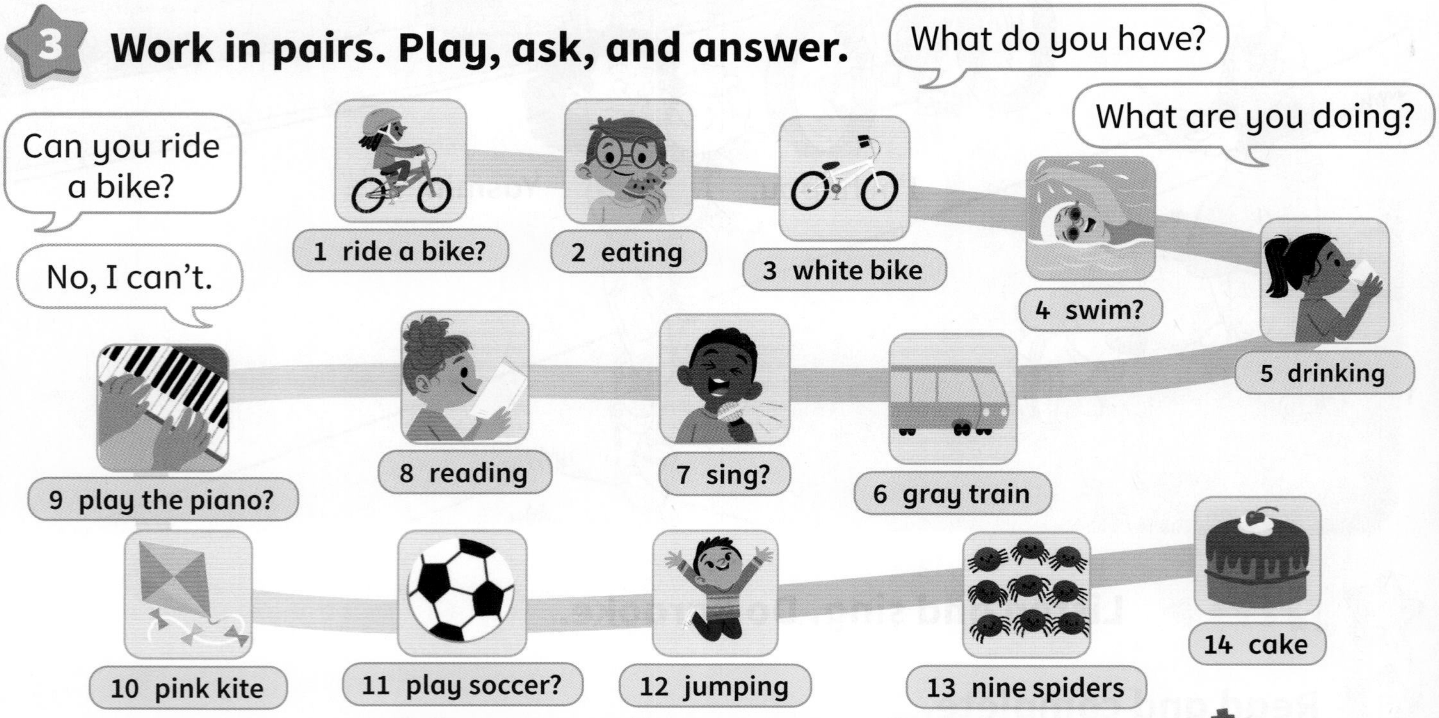

What do you have?

What are you doing?

Can you ride a bike?

No, I can't.

1 ride a bike?

2 eating

3 white bike

4 swim?

5 drinking

9 play the piano?

8 reading

7 sing?

6 gray train

10 pink kite

11 play soccer?

12 jumping

13 nine spiders

14 cake

Show what you know

The _____ paints a _____ kite.

Sounds and spelling: *i–e, y, ay, ai, ei, a–e*

1 **Describe the pictures in pairs.**

1 Family matters

Family Tree

grandparents

uncle   parents   Grandpa   Grandma

aunt

Uncle Fred   Mrs. Star   Mr. Star   Aunt May

Sally   Scott   Suzy

My family tree.

daughter/granddaughter   son/grandson   daughter/granddaughter

---

1 🎧 9 **Look, think, and answer. Listen and check.**

1 Is Sally at school?
2 Who's on the poster?
3 Does Sally have a brother?
4 How many sisters does she have?

2 Ask and answer.

1 Who's Sally's uncle?   Uncle Fred.
2 Who's Suzy's aunt?
3 Who are Scott's grandparents?
4 Who are Mrs. Star's daughters?
5 Who's Mr. Star's son?
6 Who's Grandpa Star's grandson?

LOOK

Who's Sally**'s** uncle?
Who's Suzy**'s** aunt?

3 📝 **Choose and describe. Write.**

My aunt is tall. She has black hair.

 1 🎧 10 Listen and say the letter.

He's taking a picture of his son.

Letter e.

 2 🎧 11 **Listen and complete.**

Suzy's sitting next to her …

… mom.

3 Ask and answer.

Who's playing a game with her aunt?

Sally!

STUDY

He**'s** tak**ing** a picture.
She**'s** paint**ing**.
They**'re** read**ing**.

Language: present progressive   **11**

Look and say the name.

1 Who likes riding bikes?
2 Who likes painting?

3 Who likes reading?
4 Who doesn't like taking a bath?

 Read and check.

Hi! I'm Aunt May.

Look at everyone in the yard! Sally's reading. She enjoys reading about science. She's smart, and she wants to be a doctor. Scott's wearing his helmet because he's riding his bike. He's with his uncle Fred. They love riding bikes.

Suzy wants to wash her dog. Dotty's naughty. She doesn't like taking a bath. Grandpa's laughing, and he's giving Suzy a towel. Suzy needs a towel!

Grandma's quiet. She enjoys painting. She's painting a beautiful picture of her granddaughter Sally.

 Say "yes" or "no."

 No.

1 Scott doesn't enjoy riding his bike.
2 Sally enjoys reading about science.
3 Scott doesn't wear a helmet.
4 Suzy wants to wash her doll.
5 Dotty likes taking a bath.
6 Grandma enjoys painting.

LOOK

Scott enjoys **riding** his bike.
Scott wants **to ride** his bike.

Language: simple present

 **12** ► **Read and complete with a name. Listen and check.**

Aunt May's a doctor.
She has straight black hair.
¹ Uncle Fred 's a farmer.
His beard is short and fair.
²   is quiet.
She wants to paint all day.
³   is funny,
And his curly hair is gray.
⁴   can be naughty.
He loves *Lock and Key*.
His sister ⁵   's smart,
And she doesn't like TV.
⁶   isn't quiet,
But she's very small.
Here's our family,
We really love them all.
We really love them all.

2  **13** ► **Listen and sing. Do karaoke.**

3 **Draw your family tree.**
Talk about your family.

STUDY

She's	my	aunt. grandmother.
He's		uncle. grandfather.

She's	my	mother's grandmother's father's grandfather's	daughter. sister.
He's			son. brother.

Vocabulary: appearance | Language: possessive 's   **13**

Lock's sounds and spelling

1 🎧 14 ▶ **Watch the video. Watch again and practice.**

2 **Find and underline the *er* sounds.**

> Bread, butter, burgers – what's for dinner?
> Father, mother, brother, and sister love making dinner.

3 **Work in pairs. Describe and say "yes" or "no."**

The mother is holding a flower.

No, the mother is eating a burger.

Show what you know

What's for _____ ? It's a _____ .

Are Lock and Key good detectives? Why? Why not?

How big is your family?

Listen and read. How many cousins does Sofia have? How many do you have?

My name's Sofia. This is my family. There are 11 people in my family.
That's me in the middle with my dad, my mom, my brother Felipe, and baby Elias.

On the left, you can see Uncle Victor, Grandma, and Aunt Fernanda.
On the right, you can see my adult cousins Raquel and Raul and Raul's wife, Alicia.

How old am I? Eight years old

How long is Dad's mustache? 5 cm

How tall is Uncle Victor? 183 cm

How long is baby Elias's foot? 6 cm

How tall is Grandma? 163 cm

How old is Felipe? Seven years old

How long is Mom's foot? 24 cm

2 **Use Sofia's poster to answer the questions.**

1 How many adults are there? _____8_____
2 How many children are there? _____
3 Uncle Victor is 183 cm tall. Grandma is 163 cm tall. What's the difference? _____ cm
4 How many fingers and toes do Felipe, Sofia, and Elias have in total? _____ fingers and toes
5 How many feet are there in the family? _____ feet
6 Sofia's family is going to a restaurant. Four people can sit at each table. How many tables do they need? _____ tables

3 **When do you use math in real life? Think and say.**

> I count my colored pencils.

> I share candy with my friends.

DIDYOUKNOW...?
Counting is the oldest form of math. Humans have been counting for 35,000 years!

Math: measuring | critical thinking

4 🎧 17 **Look at the chart. Listen and write the symbol.**

a	15	>	12		
b	6	___	2	=	3
c	16	___	19		
d	10	___	10	=	20
e	25	___	8	=	17
f	3	___	2	=	6

Math function	Symbol	Words
Addition	+	plus
Subtraction	–	minus
Multiplication	×	times
Division	÷	divided by
	=	equals
	>	is greater than
	<	is less than

5 **Guess and measure. Complete the table.**

	Guess!	Measure!
How tall am I?	___ cm	___ cm
How long is my foot?	___ cm	___ cm
How wide is my hand?	___ cm	___ cm
How wide is my English book?	___ cm	___ cm
How long is my hair?	___ cm	___ cm

6 📝 **Survey and measure your classmates. Complete the table in your notebook. Make sentences with "greater" and "less than."**

Name	Age	How tall … ?

Jackie is 12. Megan is 11.

12 is greater than 11. 12 > 11.

Ready to write:

Go to Workbook page 16.

Project

145 cm

185 cm

85 cm

Make a family numbers poster.

2 Home sweet home

upstairs

elevator

balcony

stairs

downstairs

basement

An apartment downtown

A house in the country

1 🎧 18 **Look, think, and answer. Listen and check.**

1 What buildings can you see?
2 What's in the room under the house?
3 Where's the apartment?
4 Does the apartment have a yard?

2 📝 **Describe your house or apartment. Then write.**

My house is in the country. It has a kitchen downstairs.

My house is downtown. It has a balcony.

3 🎧 19 **Listen and say the letter.**

 A basement

 Letter d.

Vocabulary: the home and the world around us

1 🎵🎧 20 ▶ **Listen and order.** (1 – c)

a

Upstairs, downstairs,
One floor or two.
We live here,
What about you?

b

Home is home, …. .
In an apartment or a house,
In the city or the country,
Home is home!
It's where I'm free.

c

We have a basement
Under the ground floor.
It has brown stairs
And a purple door.

d

I have an elevator.
It goes up and down.
From my balcony,
I can see the town.

2 🎵🎧 21 ▶ **Listen and sing. Do karaoke.**

3 **Find the differences.**

This house has a balcony.

This house doesn't have a balcony.

1 ▶ Look, read, and match.

1 – f

Eva moves to a new apartment

1 Today Eva and her family are moving. Two workers are carrying the wardrobe to the truck.

4 Eva's helping. She's taking a lamp upstairs. She's smiling because she can go in the elevator.

2 Her new address is 14 Park Road. It's an apartment. It's amazing!

5 The workers can't take the big wardrobe in the small elevator. They need to carry it up the stairs. It's difficult to carry.

3 Eva and her dad are helping the house cleaner clean the apartment.

6 Now they are sitting on the wardrobe. They're taking a break. They need a drink.

2 Write some words to complete the sentences about the story. You can use 1, 2, or 3 words.

1 Eva and her family ___are moving___ today.
2 The workers can't put the wardrobe in _____.
3 Eva, her dad, and the house cleaner _____ her amazing new apartment.
4 Eva's carrying a _____ in the elevator.
5 The workers need to carry _____ upstairs because the elevator is small.
6 The workers are _____ because they are hot, tired, and thirsty.

1 🎧 22 **Listen and say.**

12 13 14 15 16 17 18 19 100
20 30 40 50 60 70 80 90

2 🎧 23 **Listen and write the names.**

> May lives at number 72.

> That's pink.

23   37   100   59

_____   _____   _____   _____

64   72   85   98

_____   May   _____   _____

3 **Ask and answer.**

> What number's the house with a yellow door?

> It's number 23.

4 **Talk about where you live.**

> What's your address?

> It's 72 Elm Street.

LOOK

thir**teen** – thir**ty**
four**teen** – for**ty**
fif**teen** – fif**ty**
six**teen** – six**ty**
seven**teen** – seven**ty**
eigh**teen** – eigh**ty**
nine**teen** – nine**ty**
one **hun**dred

Lock's sounds and spelling

1 🎧 **24** ▶ Watch the video. Watch again and practice.

2 Look and find. Read and underline the sounds.

See the street where we meet.

Bees at number three and sheep at number thirteen.

Green trees in between.

3 Work in pairs. Write and say. Listen and complete.

The house is number 13. My number 13 is blue.

13   14   15   30   40   50

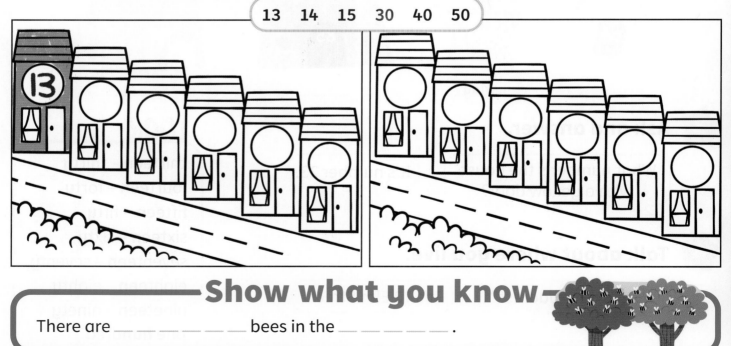

Show what you know

There are _____ bees in the _____ .

What does Mrs. Potts think about the monster? Say two things.

How are our homes unique?

1 🎧 26 **Listen and read. Which home is your favorite? Why?**

These **cabins** in Norway are on **stilts**, so they don't get wet.

These **apartments** in Singapore have colorful **spiral staircases**.

This **cave home** is in Turkey. It's very old!

Can you imagine living on a traditional Indian **houseboat**? This house can float!

This **tree house** in the U.S.A. has a **rope bridge**.

2 **Complete the chart with the words from Activity 1.**

Types of homes		Features	
cabin			

3 **What are the advantages and disadvantages of the homes in Activity 1? Think and say.**

It's in a city with stores and transportation.

It's very cold/hot.

DIDYOUKNOW...?
Some cave homes are more than 2,000 years old!

Geography: different types of homes | critical thinking

4 **Read the description of Bethany's dream bedroom. Which parts do you like the most?**

My dream bedroom

In my dream bedroom, there's a big bed. I can jump on it! I have a lot of toys. There's a slide, too. It's fast! The walls of my dream bedroom are blue. It's my favorite color! There's a spiral staircase, too. At the top, there's a special bed for my pet cat.

5 **Underline the contractions in Activity 4.**

Ready to write:

Go to Workbook page 24.

Learning to write:

Contractions

A contraction is a short form of two or more words. All contractions have an apostrophe (').

there is → there's

it is → it's

6 **You are designing your own dream bedroom. What colors and things do you want? Think and say.**

Project

Design your own dream bedroom.

wall

Review Units 1 and 2

1 Play the game.

Instructions

Elevators – Go up

Stairs – Go down

Pictures – Spell the words. If it's right, roll again. If it's wrong, stop.

2 Look, read, and answer.

1 What are the men doing?
2 What's the woman doing?
3 Which room are the family in?
4 What's the boy reading?
5 What's the girl carrying?

3 Look at the pictures. Say which one is different.

Picture *d* is different. She has short hair.

1

 a  b  c  d

2

 a 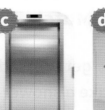 b  c d

3

 a  b  c  d

4

 a  b  c  d

Quiz

1 What's Sally's uncle's name? (p. 10)

2 What are Sally and her aunt doing? (p. 11)

3 What does Scott's grandmother love doing? (p. 12)

4 Where can you find a basement? (p. 19)

5 What are the workers carrying to Eva's apartment? (p. 20)

6 Say these numbers: 30 – 16 – 13 – 50 (p. 22)

7 Does Key want to look for Mrs. Potts's monster? (p. 23)

8 Why do some cabins have stilts? (p. 24)

3 A day in the life

1 🎧 27 Listen and say the letter. Match.

catch the bus ☐   do homework ☐   get dressed ☐   get undressed ☐
get up ☐   go to bed ☐   take a shower ☐   put on ☐
wake up [a]   take off ☐   wash ☐

2 Read and complete.

1 Sally ___wakes up___ at seven o'clock every day.
2 Before breakfast, she _____.
3 Then she gets dressed. She puts on her _____ and leggings.
4 After school, Sally does her _____.
5 She washes her _____ before dinner.
6 She _____ and takes off her T-shirt and leggings.
7 Sally goes to bed _____ nine o'clock.

3 🎧 28 Listen and do the actions.

LOOK

She wakes up at **seven o'clock**.

At **eight o'clock** she catches the bus.

1 🎵 🎧 29 ▶ Listen and match.

1 – b

I wake up in the morning.
I get up for breakfast.
I take a shower, and I get dressed. **1**
Oh, yes, every day.

I catch the bus
to take me to school.
I do my homework on the way. **2**
Oh, yes, every day.

Classes start, and
I see my teacher. **3**
Eleven o'clock, and we're out to play. **4**
Oh, yes, every day.

I wash my hands **5**
Before I have my dinner.
I get undressed, and I go to bed. **6**
Oh, yes, oh, yes,
Oh, yes, every day, every day,
every day.

2 🎵 🎧 30 ▶ Listen and sing. Do karaoke.

3 Answer the questions.

1 What time does he get dressed?
2 What time does he do his homework?
3 What time does he start school?
4 What time does he go out to play?
5 What time does he go to bed?

He gets dressed at seven o'clock.

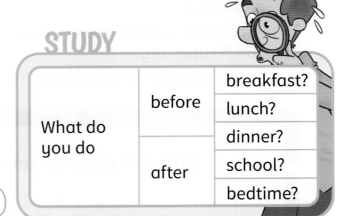

4 Ask and answer.

What do you do before breakfast?

I take a shower.

STUDY

What do you do	before	breakfast?
		lunch?
		dinner?
	after	school?
		bedtime?

 **1** 🎧 31 **Say the chant. Ask and answer.**

> What do you do on Mondays?

> I go swimming.

Monday	Tuesday	Wednesday	Thursday	Friday	Saturday/ Sunday

2 🎧 32 ▶ **Listen and say the day.**

3 🎧 33 **Listen again. Choose the right words.**

1 Scott **always** / **never** plays in the park on Mondays.
2 Scott **always** / **sometimes** does his homework on Mondays.
3 Scott **sometimes** / **never** goes swimming on Wednesdays.
4 Scott **always** / **never** plays in the park on Sundays.

STUDY

always ✓✓✓
sometimes ✓
never ✗

She **sometimes** plays soccer in the park.

He **always** wakes up at seven o'clock.

They **never** go to school on Sundays.

 Write in your notebook.

1 Scott never plays in the park on Mondays.

Vocabulary: days of the week | Language: adverbs

1 Look, read, and complete.

James Flunk is a music teacher. At school he ¹_____always_____ plays the piano, but he ²_____ plays the piano on vacation.

James loves playing tennis, so he ³_____ plays on Wednesdays. He ⁴_____ plays soccer with his daughter Jane, too. She ⁵_____ scores a goal.

Every Saturday morning, James takes his son to the swimming pool, but James ⁶_____ goes swimming.

He sometimes takes his family to the mountains on Sundays. They ⁷_____ sing songs in the car.

2 🎧 34 Listen and say "yes" or "no."

3 Look and make sentences. Use the words in the boxes.

I never ride my bike on Wednesdays.

always   sometimes   never

on Saturdays   on Wednesdays
after school   in the morning

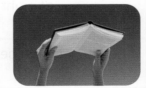

Lock's sounds and spelling

1 🎧 35 ▶ **Watch the video. Watch again and practice.**

2 **Find and underline or circle the /ɪz/, /z/, and /s/ sounds.**

Owl dances at night and plays by the moon.
He catches his food and eats before noon.

3 **Work in pairs. Write and say.**

The bee flies
to the flowers
after breakfast.

fly   dance   get up   go to bed   take a shower   wake up
wash hands   eat   brush teeth and hair   sing   do homework

before breakfast _takes a shower_	after lunch	before bed
in the morning	at night	after breakfast
after dinner	before bed	before dinner

Show what you know

The bat _____ and _____ fruit at night.

Lock & Key!

1 **Ask and answer the questions in picture 6.**

Story: unit language in context   **33**

1 🎧 37 **Listen and say. Who is Sally? Where does she live?**

Everything floats in space – even our food!

2 🎧 37 **Listen again and mark (✓) the true sentences.**

1 There are other astronauts on the space station. ☐
2 Sally works on the space station. ☐
3 Sally wears a spacesuit. ☐
4 A robot cleaner does the chores, like cleaning. ☐
5 Sally watches movies in her free time. ☐

3 **Think about the astronaut's day. How is your day similar or different? Think and say.**

I have breakfast, too.

My food doesn't float.

DIDYOUKNOW...?
There are no showers on the space station, but there are toilets!

Science: astronauts in space | 🛡 learning to learn

4 Read Sally's blog. What is special about today?

www.myspaceblog.com

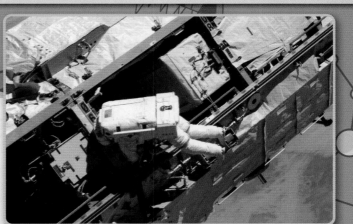

24 June

Today is my first spacewalk. I'm so excited!

I get up at six o'clock, and I wash.

At half past six, I have breakfast. Eggs and bread! Yum!

Then, I put on my spacesuit. Another astronaut helps me, and it takes a long time.

Now it's nine o'clock. The doors open, and I go outside. Wow! I have an amazing view of Earth!

5 Underline the times in Activity 4.

Ready to write:

Go to Workbook page 34.

Learning to write:

Times

six o'clock   half past six   nine o'clock

6 Prepare for an interview with an astronaut. What questions do you want to ask?

Project

1 Do you sleep in a bed?

2

Role-play an interview with an astronaut.

4 In the city

1 What are they looking at? Why?

2 🎧 38 Listen. Find Eva's apartment.
Match and write the number in the box.

bank ☐ bus station ☐ movie theater ☐ sports center ☐
supermarket ☐ swimming pool ☐ library ☐ market ☐ 1

3 Ask and answer. *What's across from the movie theater?* *The bus station.*

in front of

behind

next to

between

across from

Vocabulary: places | **Language:** prepositions of place

 **39** **Look at the picture. Listen and answer.**

> Where's the park?

> It's in front of the swimming pool.

2 **Ask and answer.**

> Where's the trash can?

> It's in front of the hotel.

3 **Read and complete with the words from the picture in Activity 1.**

This is a picture of my town. Look at the ¹ swimming pool across from the park.
I sometimes go there to swim with Sally. We always take our swimsuits and
towels with us. We go to the ² _____ to buy our food. It's between
the bank and the ³ _____. Where do my parents go to get money?
They go to the ⁴ _____. Can you see the ⁵ _____? I go there
to catch the bus to school. Where do I love going on Saturdays? I love going
to the ⁶ _____ to see a movie. It's my favorite place in the town. When
my grandparents come to town, they stay in the ⁷ _____.

4  **40** **Listen and answer.**

> Where do you go to see a movie?

> I go to the movie theater to see a movie.

Language: prepositions of place and infinitive of purpose   37

 **Look, think, and answer. Listen and check.**

1 Where are the children?
2 Which children are happy?

3 What book does Robert have?
4 What time is it?

2  42 **Listen and say "yes" or "no."**

3 **Ask and answer.**

When do you go to the library?

I go to the library on Saturdays.

1 When do you go to the library?
2 What do you enjoy reading?
3 When do you read?
4 Does your family read?
5 Why do you read?

STUDY

Scott **has to** be quiet in the library.
They **have to** catch the bus.
She **has to** do her homework.

Language: *have/has to* for obligation

1  43 ▶ Read and match. Listen and check. 1 – d

1 Do I have to make my bed?	Yes, you do.
2 Do I have to wear a skirt?	Yes, you do.
3 Do I have to go to school?	Yes, you do.
4 Do I have to do my homework?	Yes, you do.
5 Do I have to clean my shoes?	Yes, you do.
6 Can I play in the park, Dad?	Yes, you can!

2  44 ▶ Listen and sing. Do karaoke.

3 Ask and answer.

make the bed   clean your room
clean your shoes   help in the kitchen
wash the car   help Mom and Dad

What do you have to do at home?

I have to clean my room.

1  45 ▶ **Watch the video. Watch again and practice.**

2 **Find and circle the sounds. Say.**

LIBRARY

Where's the bear with purple hair?
He's over there, on the chair!

3 **Draw lines. Then ask, answer, and draw.**

Where's the small bear?

The small bear is in the bank.

Show what you know

There's a small _____ with yellow _____ .

Lock & Key!

1 Where does Mrs. Potts have to go? Why?

Where do we go shopping?

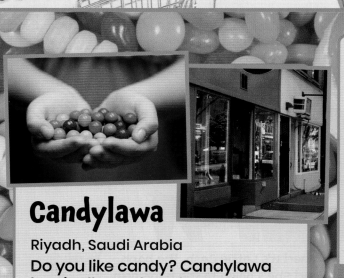

Candylawa

Riyadh, Saudi Arabia

Do you like candy? Candylawa has it all: candy, cake, and popcorn. After buying some treats, you can buy nice gifts, such as T-shirts and animal toys. There's also a café for visitors.

Brooklyn Superhero Supply Company

New York City, U.S.A.

Are you a superhero? Do you want to be one? This store has superhero costumes, such as masks and capes. You can also buy fun toys and science kits to make things! You can build a robot or write a secret message with invisible ink.

2 **Read and match. Then write.**

		What do both stores sell?
Brooklyn Superhero Supply Company	**a** in Saudi Arabia	
	b in the U.S.A.	
Candylawa	**c** costumes	
	d a café	
	e sweet treats	

3 **What stores do you like? What do you buy there? Think and say.**

> I like craft stores.

> I buy paint and crayons.

DIDYOUKNOW...?
Clothes and shoes are the most popular items for online shopping.

Geography: shopping | 🛡 critical thinking

Why are these stores different? Read and match.

1

MOVING BOOKS

Imagine a van that drives around and sells books! You can buy books in a field or in a parking lot. Books about space, storybooks, notebooks — you can find them all here!

2

COCONUT DELIGHT

Thirsty? Come and drink some delicious coconut water. You can find us by the beach.

3

C+M ice cream

Can you hear the music? The ice cream truck is coming!! It drives to your street or your school, and you can buy yummy ice cream.

5 Underline the nouns in Activity 4.

Learning to write:

Nouns

A noun is a word for a person, place, or thing.

6 Imagine you want to open a store. What do you sell? Think and say.

Ready to write:

Go to Workbook page 42.

Project

Role-play a conversation at your store.

Review Units 3 and 4

1 Play the game.

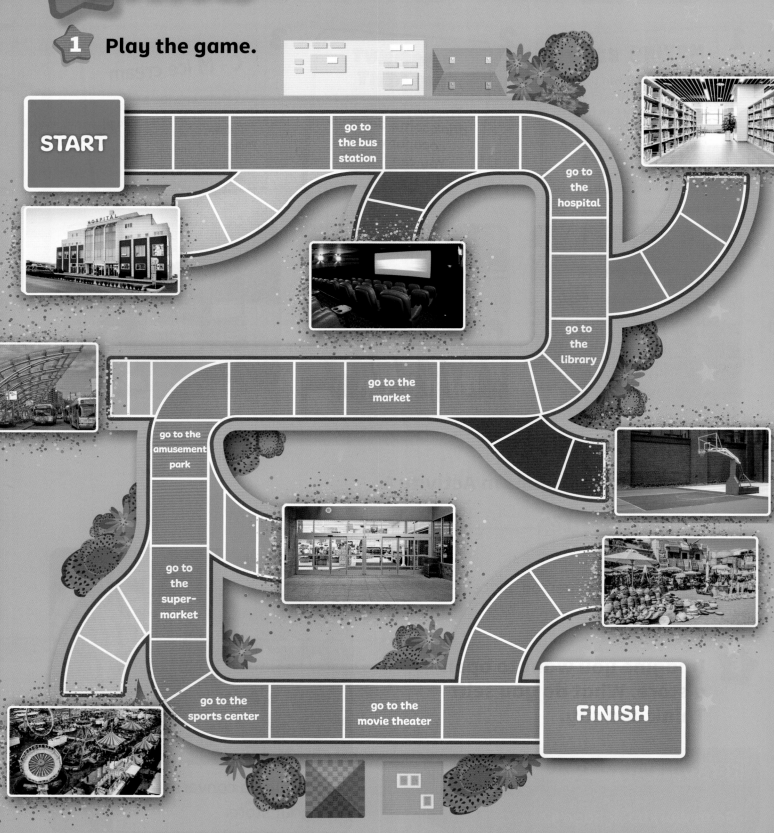

START

go to
the bus
station

go to
the
hospital

go to
the
library

go to the
market

go to the
amusement
park

go to
the
super-
market

go to the
sports center

go to the
movie theater

FINISH

 **48**

Listen and choose the correct picture.

 **Quiz**

1 What does Jack do on Saturdays?

a    b  Movie theater TODAY ✓   c

2 What time does Daisy come home from school?

a    b 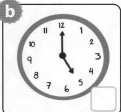   c

3 What does Paul do after dinner?

a    b    c

4 Where does Vicky catch the bus?

a    b 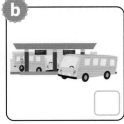   c  SUPERMARKET

5 Where's John going?

a  LIBRARY   b  HOSPITAL   c  Books

1 What time does Sally catch the bus to school? (p. 28)

2 What does James Flunk do every Saturday morning? (p. 31)

3 Do Lock and Key get up before ten o'clock? (p. 33)

4 Where does Sally the astronaut work? (p. 34)

5 On Eva's map, what's across from the market? (p. 36)

6 Where do you go to see a movie? (p. 37)

7 Where's the bear with the purple hair? (p. 40)

8 Why do Mrs. Potts and her friend have to go to the bank? (p. 41)

5 Stay healthy

a temperature   a cold   a cough   a headache   a toothache   a stomachache

1 🎧 49 **Look, think, and answer. Listen and check.**

1 Where are Sally and Scott?
2 Who's the doctor?

3 Is Sally hot?
4 Is Scott sick?

2 **What's the matter? Act it out.**

What's the matter?

He has a cough/stomachache.

3 🎧 50 **Listen and do the actions.**

STUDY

What's the matter?
He **has** a cough.
She **has** a temperature.
I **have** a stomachache.

Vocabulary: illness | **Language:** *have* and *has*

1 🎧 51 Listen and say the letter.

 a
 b
 c
 d

 e
 f
 g
 h

2 Make sentences. Say the letter.

He She They	has have	a toothache. a backache. a stomachache. a headache.	an earache. a temperature. a cold. a cough.

She has an earache.

d

3 Read and say "yes" or "no."

Poor Sally! Her head hurts, and she's very hot. She has a temperature. She isn't feeling very well because she has a cough and a bad cold. She has to stay in bed and drink a lot of water and orange juice. She's sad because she wants to go to school, but she can't.

Scott shouldn't eat candy or chocolate today because he says he has a stomachache. Do you think he has a stomachache, or do you think he's OK?

1 Sally's back hurts.
2 She has a temperature.
3 She has to stay in bed.
4 She has to drink a lot of orange juice.
5 Scott says he has a toothache.
6 He has to eat candy and chocolate today.

4 Work in pairs. Say and guess.

My stomach hurts.

You have a stomachache.

 **1** 🎧 52 ▶ **Look, think, and answer. Listen and check.**

1 Where's Sally?

2 Who's Mrs. Star talking to?

3 What's the matter with Sally?

4 Can she go to school?

2 📝 **Make more sentences.**

> Sally has to stay in bed.
> Sally shouldn't get up.

3 🎧 53 **Listen and say "shouldn't" or "have to."**

When you have a cough, you ... go out.

shouldn't

When you have a headache, you ... go to bed.

have to

STUDY

You **have to** stay in bed.
She **shouldn't** go out.

Language: *have/has to* and *shouldn't* for obligation

1 Read the story. Look at the pictures. Write the correct word next to numbers 1–6.

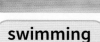
swimming

cough

bed

school

sleep

doctor

It's Tuesday, and Paul's at home. He can't go to ¹ __school__ because he's sick. He has a temperature. He shouldn't get up. He has to stay in bed. He has a ² _____ and a cold. His ³ _____ says he shouldn't run or play. He has to ⁴ _____ and drink a lot. Paul always has a ⁵ _____ lesson on Tuesdays, but he can't go today. He isn't sad because he can listen to music in ⁶ _____ !

2 🎵🎧 54 ▶ **Listen and move.**

swim

skip

jump

hop

climb

run

dance

Move, move, move
To be healthy and well.
Come on move your body!

Let's have a good time.
Run, swim, and climb.
Move, move, move,
Move your body!

Dance, dance, dance.
Don't stop until you drop.
Come on, you know it's fun!

Dance, dance, dance.
Hop, skip, and jump.
Come on, you know it's fun!

Let's have a good time ...

3 🎵🎧 55 ▶ **Listen and sing. Do karaoke.**

Vocabulary: sports and free time   49

1 🎧 56 ▶ **Watch the video. Watch again and practice.**

2 📝 **Listen and write.**

He has a cold, and he's feeling sick – poor farmer Rick!
The sheep have stomachaches – they ate a lot of cake.

3 **Work in pairs. Describe and say.**

She has a toothache.   She shouldn't eat candy.

Show what you know

The rabbits _____ coughs, and she _____ a cold.

1 **How many kinds of cake does Key have? What are they?**

What remedies do we use?

1 🎧 58 **Listen and read. Do you use any of these remedies? Do you think they work?**

What do you do when you're sick? Here are some common home remedies!

Soup – Do you have a cold or the flu? Chicken soup is a famous food remedy. In some countries, lizard soup is popular!

Herbal tea – Hot tea is a popular remedy. Herbal teas come from different parts of plants. Do you have a sore throat or stomachache? These teas can help you.

Essential oils – Essential oils come from plants, too. You can use essential oils on your skin for headaches and muscle aches. But be careful! One or two drops is enough.

REMEMBER!
Water's always good for you!

2 **Look and suggest a remedy from the text. Write your answer on the lines.**

essential oils _____ _____ _____

_____ _____ _____ _____

3 **What other home remedies or health advice can you think of? Say.**

Take vitamin C.

Stay in bed.

Put ice on it.

DID YOU KNOW...?
Most remedies come from plants – about 70%!

4 **Read the brochure. What is the problem? How can you treat it?**

Help! I have the hiccups!

Hiccup facts

Hiccups can happen when you're cold or when you eat too fast.

Hiccups come from muscle movements. They cause you to make a "hiccup" noise. You can't control the hiccups.

How to treat the hiccups

✓ Hold your breath and count to ten.
✓ Eat a spoonful of honey or sugar.

✗ Don't worry. Hiccups usually stop after a few minutes.

5 **Underline the imperative verbs in Activity 4.**

Learning to write:

Imperatives

<u>Count</u> to ten. <u>Don't worry</u>.

Ready to write:

Go to Workbook page 52.

6 **In pairs, give examples of other illnesses. Complete the table in your notebook.**

Illness	Do	Don't
toothache		

Project

Make a class book of remedies.

6 A day in the country

leaf/leave

field   picnic

plant

waterfall

grass

rock   forest

lake   river

1 🎧 59 **Look, think, and answer. Listen and check.**

1 Where do they want to go?
2 Does Mr. Star want to play tennis?

3 What does Scott want to do?
4 What does Sally want to do?

2 🎧 60 **Listen and say the letter.**   Forest.   Letter e.

3 **Ask and answer.**

What do you want to do in the country?

I want to have a picnic and swim in the river.

Read and complete.

 6

A picnic without bread

Charlie and his sister Lily enjoy having picnics in the country. Today they're having a picnic in the forest with their grandmother.

Charlie and his grandmother are sitting on a blanket. They're putting the picnic on it. After lunch, Charlie wants to do his homework. He has to look at the plants and draw their leaves.

Charlie looks sad because the bread's very old and they can't eat it for lunch.

Lily's standing next to the lake. She looks happy because she's throwing bread to the ducks. It isn't the bread for the ducks, it's the new bread for their picnic.

The ducks are eating the family's lunch!

1 Today Charlie and Lily are eating lunch in …
2 … wants to draw the plants and their leaves.
3 Charlie doesn't like his bread because …
4 Lily isn't sitting … with her brother and grandmother.
5 She's giving the new bread to …
6 The ducks are having … for lunch!

> Today Charlie and Lily are eating lunch in the forest.

 **Complete the story.
Use the words in the box.**

> forest   ~~picnics~~   old   blanket
> grandmother   his   lake
> eat   picnic   ducks

Charlie and Lily like going for ¹ _picnics_ in the country. Today they are in the ² _____ with their grandmother. Charlie and ³ _____ ⁴ _____ are putting the food on the ⁵ _____ . Charlie's looking at the bread because it's ⁶ _____ , so they can't ⁷ _____ it. Next to the ⁸ _____ , Lily's throwing bread to the ⁹ _____ . It's the nice new bread for the family's ¹⁰ _____ !

1 … puts the table under a tree.
2 … helps Scott.
3 … wants some food.
4 … isn't happy with her drawing.

2 🎧 62 **Close your books. Listen and answer.**

3 Mime and guess. Are you thirsty? Yes, I am.

LOOK

Should I help you with the blanket?

Yes, please.

1 🎵🎧 63 ▶ **Read and complete. Listen and check.**

bad   hair   long   quiet   tall   ~~thin~~

People, people, here or there.
People, people, everywhere.
Different colors, different skin.
Bodies that are fat, bodies that are ¹ thin .

Some are weak, some are strong.
With hair that's short, or hair that's ² .
Straight, curly, dark, or fair.
Different people, different ³ .

People, different people, different.
Hungry, thirsty, happy, or sad.
Young or old, good or ⁴ .
People are big, people are small.
People are short, people are ⁵ .

People, different people, different.
Funny, naughty, angry, or tired.
Smart, beautiful, loud, or ⁶ .
People, people, here or there.
People, people, everywhere.

2 🎵🎧 64 ▶ **Listen and sing. Do karaoke.**

3 🎧 65 **Listen and write. Match the words and the pictures.**

1 A-N-G-R-Y   Angry – d.

Vocabulary: adjectives   **57**

 # Lock's sounds and spelling

1 🎧 66 ▶ **Watch the video. Watch again and practice.**

In the forest, parrots sit on the grass by the river. They watch their bread and grapes so crocodiles can't steal their dinner.

2 **Listen and write.**

3 **Look, ask, and answer.** (What's the big crocodile doing?) (It's sitting by the river.)

Show what you know

The _____ is swimming in the _____.

Lock & Key!

1 **Describe the pictures. What are they doing?**

Why do we live in different places?

1 🎧 68   **Listen and read. Which place do you prefer? Why?**

City: Singapore

Hi! I'm Tara. I'm a teenager, and I live in Singapore. I love my city because it's really big and there's a lot to do. I live on the 36th floor, and from my window I can see stores and the skatepark. The city is great, but I think there's a lot of traffic and pollution, and that isn't good for us.

Country: Argentina

Hello, I'm Emilio. I live in the country in Argentina because my dad's a farm worker. My mom's English, and she's a writer. I like my life in the country because it's quiet and we have a big yard with apple trees. I love nature, but sometimes it's a little boring because I don't meet many people and it's difficult to make friends. All my friends live far away!

2   **Read and put a check mark in the correct column.**

		City	Country
1	People have more space to live.		✓
2	The air isn't clean.		
3	There's less noise.		
4	There's more public transportation.		
5	People can enjoy nature more.		

3   **What are the advantages and disadvantages of living in the city? Think and say.**

It's very noisy.   Disadvantage!

DIDYOUKNOW...?
Most people in the world live in towns and cities – about 60%!

4 Read the emails. Underline the advantages of each place in green and the disadvantages in red.

Dear Metin,

I'm Ruby, and I'm from Australia. I live in the outback in a small town called Kemble Creek.

I love living in the country because I like riding horses. My horse is named Zara, and she loves it when we ride out to visit my aunt. I don't see my friends a lot because they live far away.

Please write soon!

Ruby

Hi Ruby,

I'm Metin. I'm a teenager, and I live in Istanbul. It's a huge city with a lot to do. I go skateboarding in the park with my friends every day.

I live with my sister, Defne, and my mom. My mom is a construction worker!

I love the city, but there's a lot of pollution. I don't like that!

Take care,

Metin

5 Circle the capital letters in names and places in Activity 4.

Ready to write:

Go to Workbook page 65.

Learning to write:

Capitalization

I'm **L**eo. I live in **N**ew **Y**ork.

6 **In pairs, say the advantages and disadvantages of your city or town. Complete the table in your notebook.**

I live in _____	
Advantages of living here	**Disadvantages of living here**

Project

Do an interview on life in the city or the country.

Review Units 5 and 6

1 Play the game.

START

1

2

3 You shouldn't swim in the lake. Go back 2.

4

5 You can cross the bridge. Go forward 2.

6 Your feet are wet. Go back 2.

7

8 It's dark. You have to go forward 1.

9

10 You have to roll a six and roll again to climb the mountain and continue.

11

12 You can walk in this field. Go forward 2.

13

14

15 There's a forest. You have to miss a turn.

16

17

18 You can't find your hat. Go back 2.

19

20 You want to go home. Roll again.

21

22

23

24 You can see the car. Go forward 1.

25

26 You take a photo of a waterfall. Go back 3.

FINISH

2 Find eight more differences.

In picture 1, there are five bananas. In picture 2, there are four bananas.

3 Choose the correct words. Say.

chocolate

a field

a river

a temperature

a picnic

a headache

a blanket

1 Cows and sheep sometimes live here. *A field.*
2 Fish can swim here.
3 Charlie has a toothache. He shouldn't eat this.
4 This is when your head hurts.
5 You have this when you aren't feeling well and you're very hot.
6 You put this on your bed when you're cold.

Quiz

1 Why does Sally have to go to bed? (p. 46)

2 What's the matter with Paul? (p. 49)

3 What's Miss Rich's beautiful painting called? (p. 51)

4 What are Lily and her family doing in the forest? (p. 55)

5 Is Suzy hungry or thirsty? (p. 56)

6 Where do Lock and Key want to go for a picnic? (p. 59)

7 What's an advantage of living in the city? (p. 60)

8 Where does Ruby live? (p. 61)

7 World of animals

1 🎧 69 **Look, think, and answer. Listen and check.**

1 What are Scott and Sally doing?
2 Which animals are strong?
3 Which animal does Sally like?
4 Which animals talk a lot?

2 **Ask and answer.**

Which animals do you like?

Where do they live?

I like pandas.

They live in the forests and mountains in China.

3 🎧 70 **Complete. Listen and check.**

night   sleep
~~ocean~~   leaves   meat

1 Dolphins, jellyfish, whales, and sharks live in the ___ocean___ .
2 Bears eat fish, fruit, plants, and _____ .
3 Kangaroos eat _____ .
4 Lions are strong, and they _____ a lot.
5 Bats sleep in the day and get their food at _____ .

64   Vocabulary: animals

Read and match.

 a
 b
 c
 d
 e

 f
 g
 h
 i
 j

1 This huge gray animal lives in the ocean. It has a very big mouth and a lot of teeth. It can sometimes eat people. ☐ e

2 This gray animal lives in the ocean. It has a long nose and small teeth. It's very smart, and it likes playing. ☐

3 This big brown animal lives in Australia. It has two long, strong legs and two short, thin arms. It can jump. ☐

4 This animal can fly. It eats fruit. It can be red, green, and blue, and it's very loud. ☐

5 This big animal is gray, brown, or white. It's big, and it can stand on two legs. It eats fish, meat, fruit, and plants. It sleeps when it's cold. ☐

6 This black and white bird can swim, but it can't fly. It lives in very cold climates, and it eats fish. ☐

 Play the game.

(This animal has a long nose and small teeth.)   (It's a dolphin.)

 Read and complete with the words in the box.

(eats   cold   sometimes   ~~huge~~   gray   ocean   animals)

This ¹ _huge_ blue or ² _____ animal lives in the ³ _____ .
It likes very ⁴ _____ water. It ⁵ _____ a lot of small
⁶ _____ and plants. It's ⁷ _____ very long.

Vocabulary: animals   65

1 🎧 71 ▶ **Look and answer. Listen and check.**

1 Who's doing a project on animals?

2 Which two animals are they looking at?

3 Can bats carry trees?

4 Are elephants strong?

 2 **What do you think?**
Read and say "yes" or "no."

1 Whales are bigger than penguins.

2 Dolphins are longer than whales.

3 Lions are faster than pandas.

4 Bats are dirtier than elephants.

5 Jellyfish are better at climbing than pandas.

6 Sharks are worse at swimming than kangaroos.

STUDY

Regular:

clean + er – clean**er**

big + g + er – big**ger**

dirty – y + ier – dirt**ier**

Irregular:

good – **better**

bad – **worse**

Language: comparative adjectives

 **72** ► **Listen and complete. Sing the song.**

 7

~~bigger~~ see me hiding snake smaller can than

I'm walking,
I'm walking.
What can I see?
I can see a lion, and it's ¹ **bigger**
than me!

I'm swimming,
I'm swimming.
What can I see?
I ² _____ see a shark,
and it's uglier ³ _____ me!

I'm standing,
I'm standing.
What can I see?
I can see a ⁴ _____,
and it's thinner than me!

I'm hiding,
I'm ⁵ _____.
What can I see?
I can see a bat,
and it's ⁶ _____ than me!

I'm sitting,
I'm sitting.
What can I see?
I can ⁷ _____ a monkey,
and it's naughtier than ⁸ _____!

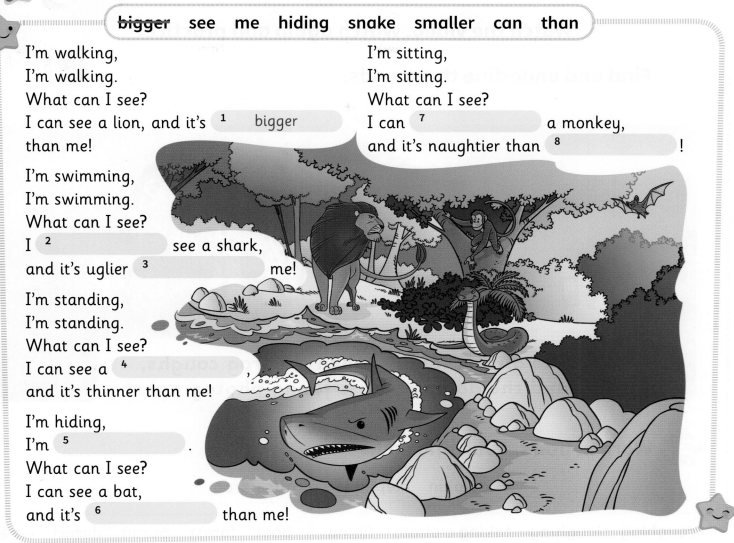

2 🎵🎧 **73** ► **Listen and sing. Do karaoke.**

3 **Make sentences. Use the words in the boxes.**

> The cat's weaker than the lion.

  quiet strong weak

 long big

  fat slow

 bad/good at jumping

Language: comparative adjectives and present progressive   67

Lock's sounds and spelling

1 🎧 74 ▶ **Watch the video. Watch again and practice.**

2 **Find and underline the sounds.**

> **The giraffe laughs when the frog coughs, and the dolphin takes funny photographs!**

3 **Work in pairs. Look and say.**

dolphin   elephant   giraffe   frog

coughing   laughing   taking a photo   flying   boat   forest   ocean   desert   tree

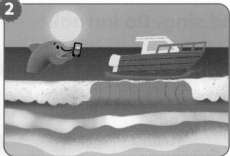

> In the ocean, there's a dolphin with a phone.

> Number 2!

Show what you know

The _____ takes a _____ of the _____.

Why does Key think the man isn't Robin Motors? Say 5 things.

How do animals stay safe?

1 🎧 76 **Listen and read. Which animal is bad for birds?**

Grasshoppers are green, yellow, and brown. They use camouflage, so animals can't see them in the grass. They can jump with their big legs to escape from other animals.

Hummingbirds are very small. They have bright colors. They can fly very fast, so other animals can't catch them.

Monarch butterflies have orange and black wings. They can fly. They're poisonous to birds.

Sea turtles are green, brown, or black. They live in the ocean. They can swim. They have hard shells, so other animals can't eat them.

2 **Read again and complete the chart.**

animals	colors	How do they stay safe?
grasshoppers	green, yellow, and 1 _____	They use camouflage. They can jump.
monarch 2 _____	orange and 3 _____	They're 4 _____ to birds.
hummingbirds	bright colors	They can fly very 5 _____ .
sea turtles	green, brown, or black	They have hard 6 _____ .

3 **Work in pairs. Say and guess.**

It has big legs.

A grasshopper!

DIDYOUKNOW...?
Octopuses can change color to have better camouflage.

4 Read the description of the imaginary animal. What can you say about the animal?

This is a "hippoctopus." It's part hippo, part octopus. It lives in the ocean. It's pink and orange. It has big teeth to scare away sharks. It eats starfish. It can swim fast.

5 Circle the adjectives in Activity 4.

Learning to write:

Adjectives
It is <u>pink</u> and <u>orange</u>.
It has <u>bright</u> colors.

Ready to write:

Go to Workbook page 70.

6 Combine two animals and invent a name. What features does it have?

It's part zebra, part parrot. It's a zebrot! It has the colorful wings of a parrot.

Project

<u>Eleraffe</u>
It's an elephant and a giraffe. It has giraffe legs.

Write a fact file for an imaginary animal.

8 Weather report

Dear Eva,
We're on vacation in the country.
It's windy, and we can fly our kites.
It's very wet, too. It's raining now.
It rains every day here!
Scott and Sally

Dear Scott,
I'm on vacation at the beach.
It's hot and sunny! It's very
dry here because it isn't
raining. Look at me in my
swim trunks!
Robert

Dear Grandma
and Grandpa,
We're on vacation at the
lakes with Dotty. It's cloudy,
but I can see a rainbow!
It's really beautiful.
Suzy

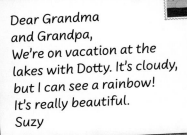

Dear Sally,
I'm on vacation in the
mountains. It's great!
It's cold, and there's a
lot of snow. Look at
my snowman!
Eva

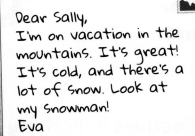

1 Ask and answer. Look and check.

1 Who has a pet?
2 Where's Eva on vacation?
3 Who's on vacation in the country?
4 Where's Robert on vacation?

2 Look and say the name.

It's windy.   Scott and Sally!

3 🎧 77 Listen and say "yes" or "no."

1
2
3
4
5
6

Vocabulary: weather

1 🎧 78 **Listen and match.**   1 – snowing

windy

1

snowing

raining

sunny

rainbow

cloudy

2 🎧 79 **Listen and complete.**

1 It's _____ in the mountains.
2 In the forest, it's _____ .
3 It's _____ on the island.
4 It's _____ and _____ at the lake.
5 At the beach, it's very _____ .
6 You can see a _____ near the fields.

3 **Ask and answer.**

What's the weather like at the beach?   It's windy.

a

b

c

d

e

Language: *What's the weather like? It's (windy).*   **73**

1 🎧 80 ▶ Look, think, and answer. Listen and check.

1 Who's Alex talking to?
2 Who's Alex with?
3 Where's Alex today?
4 Is the weather cold today?

yesterday

today

2 🎧 81 Listen and say "yesterday" or "today."

3 Ask and answer.

Where were you yesterday evening?

I was at the sports center.

STUDY

It **was** wet and windy yesterday.
They **were** out yesterday.
It**'s** hot and sunny today.
They **are** at home today.

Language: simple past – *was* and *were*

1  82 ▶ Read and complete. Listen and check.

coat   cold   hat   scarf   snow   sweater   windy

, coat, sweater, and scarf.

It was cold and  in the park, cold and windy!

It was gray and cloudy.

There wasn't any sun.

There weren't many children, it wasn't much fun.

Hat, 🧥, sweater, and scarf.

It was 🧣 and windy in the park, cold and windy!

There wasn't a rainbow.

There wasn't any ❄.

Grandpa and I were ready to go.

Hat, coat, sweater, and 🧣.

It was cold and windy in the park, cold and windy!

Back at home,

It was much better

With a hot drink and my big red 🧥.

🧢, coat, sweater, and scarf.

It was cold and 🌬 in the park, cold and windy!

Windy in the park!

2 🎵🎧 83 ▶ Listen and sing. Do karaoke.

3 Make sentences.

It was hot and sunny. He was in a T-shirt and swim trunks.

It was cold and windy. His gloves were gray, and his scarf was blue.

sunny   rainy   snowy   dry   wet   hot   cold   swim trunks   T-shirt   gloves   coat   scarf

Lock's sounds and spelling

1 🎧 84 ▶ **Watch the video. Watch again and practice.**

2 📝 **Listen and write.**

In the sunny sky, bees dance, and parrots fly.
A giraffe's over there sitting on a red chair.
He watches the bear paint frogs with no hair.

3 **Work in pairs. Say and guess.**

I was in a T-shirt. I was next to a jellyfish in the ocean.

You were at the beach. It was sunny and dry!

Show what you know

The _____ paints _____ on a _____ day.

Sounds and spelling: *y, ee, r, s, ff, ere, air, es, ear, ai, f*

8

Lock & Key!

85 ▶

1

Key! The police have Robin motors! Let's go to the police station to ask him some questions.

I don't think it was him, Lock.

2

Are you cold, Lock? No problem. We can go in the car.

But we don't have a car now, and it's raining!

3

So, mr. motors. Where were you last Thursday morning?

Thursday morning? At what time?

At eleven o'clock.

4

You were on Baker Street at eleven o'clock last Thursday morning.

No, I wasn't.

Oh, yes, you were.

5

YOU WERE IN MY CAR LAST THURSDAY MORNING!

No, mr. Lock, he was here at the police station.

6

That was my brother, Nick motors.

I was right! It wasn't Robin motors!

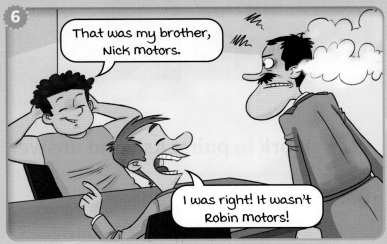

1 **Work in pairs. Describe the pictures.**

In picture 1, Lock's happy.

Story: unit language in context   77

What does nature sound like?

1 🎧 86 **Listen. What do the instruments sound like?**

animals   insects   rain   thunder

a
_____

b
_____

c
_____

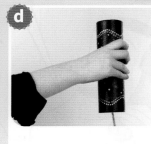
d
_____

2 🎧 87 **Listen and write "wind" or "percussion."**

b **Instrument:** rain stick

Family of instruments:
percussion

Country: Chile

Sounds like: rain

☐ **Instrument:** vuvuzela

Family of instruments:
_____

Country: South Africa

Sounds like: insects

☐ **Instrument:** thunder drum

Family of instruments:
_____

Country: Indonesia

Sounds like: thunder

☐ **Instrument:** didgeridoo

Family of instruments:
_____

Country: Australia

Sounds like: Australian animals

3 **Work in pairs. Ask and answer.**

What country is the vuvuzela from?

South Africa.

DIDYOUKNOW...?
The Sea Organ is a musical instrument that you don't need to play. Waves make the music.

Music: sounds in nature | 🛡 learning to learn

4 Read the invitation. What is the event? What do you need to know about it?

You're invited!

Come to our nature sounds concert! You can hear musical instruments that sound like thunder and rain. Make your own instruments, too!

Date: Saturday, May 14

Time: 4 pm

Place: Kyle's backyard

RSVP: Please message us at 0786547112 to let us know you're coming. See you on Saturday!

Kyle and friends

5 Underline the key information with the correct colors.

What? Where? When?

Learning to write:

Key information
What? Where? When?

6 📝 **In groups, list musical instruments you have or can make. Who's going to play each instrument?**

Name	Instrument

Project

Plan a musical event and make a poster.

Ready to write:

Go to Workbook page 78.

Review Units 7 and 8

1 Play the game.

Instructions

1 Play in pairs.
2 Choose:
  - weather and clothes
  - animals
  - in town
  - in the country
3 Write the topic and the 7 words in your notebook.

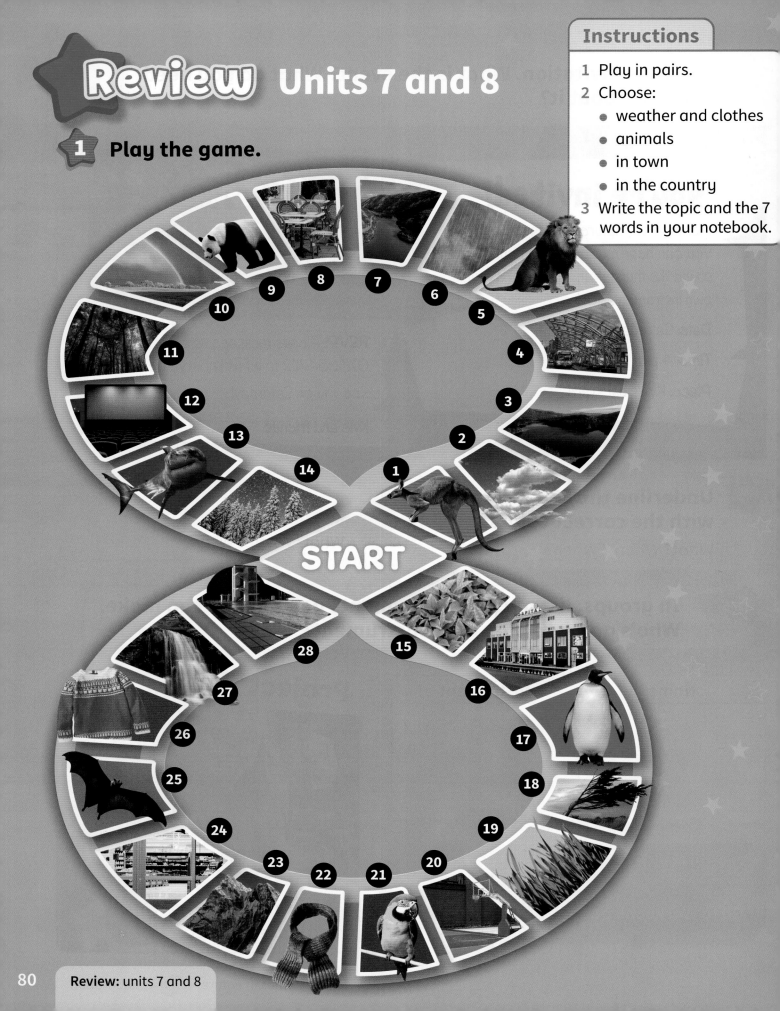

START

2 🎧 88 **Listen and draw lines. There is one example.**

Daisy _____   Anna _____   Beth _____

Jack _f_   Abdul _____   Zak _____

Quiz

1 What 3 animals are in the ocean? (p. 64)

2 This bird can swim, but it can't fly. What is it? (p. 65)

3 Where do Lock and Key go for a cold drink? (p. 69)

4 Where was Eva on vacation? (p. 72)

5 What was the weather like at the park, and what was Grandpa wearing? (p. 75)

6 Say all the different sounds on page 76.

7 Where was Robin Motors last Thursday morning? (p. 77)

8 What instrument is played by the waves of the ocean? (p. 78)

1 🎧 89 **Look and complete. Listen and check.**

1 The boys' clothes are too _____ .
2 Ana can eat the _____ they planted.
3 The children are painting the _____ .
4 The children are putting _____ into the boxes.

2 **Read and correct.**

1 They share toys with other people.
2 The children are planting flowers in the community garden.
3 The children are painting the wall red.
4 The children are putting the food in the cupboard.
5 The boys want to keep their clothes.
6 One person eats the food from the community garden.

3 **Think and discuss. What do you share?**

I share a computer with my brother.

1 🎧 90 **Look and think. Say "yes" or "no." Listen and check.**

1 In the city, it's OK to throw trash on the ground.
2 It's OK to park your car next to a "No parking" sign.
3 On the train, it's OK not to give your seat to an older person who needs to sit down.
4 In a park, it's OK to play soccer next to the flowers.

2 **Read and match.**   (1 – b)

1 Don't break flowers …
2 You can put your …
3 You can park …
4 On trains and buses, don't …
5 Don't park next to …
6 You can help to make your …

a … sit in seats that are for older people.
b … and trees in the park.
c … trash in the trash can.
d … town clean and beautiful.
e … the "No parking" sign.
f … in the parking lot.

3 **Think and discuss. What can you do to help your town?**

I can have a picnic in the park and put my trash in the trash can.

1 🎧 91 Look, read, and match. Listen and check.

1 You shouldn't be angry when you don't win.
2 In sports, you have to help other players.
3 In sports, it is good to learn new skills.
4 When you play sports, you need to know the rules.

2 Read and correct.

1 We shouldn't be friendly to the other players.
2 You never have to follow the rules of the game.
3 When we play sports, it's always important to win.
4 Don't help other players.
5 It isn't important to enjoy playing sports.
6 We have to be angry when we don't win.

3 Think and discuss. Is it important to play or to win? Why?

> I think it's important to play because I can learn new things.

1 🎧 92 **Look and think. Say "yes" or "no." Listen and check.**

1 If you live near your school, you can sometimes walk there.
2 When you brush your teeth, you can turn the water off.
3 You shouldn't take bags with you when you go shopping.
4 You never need to turn computers or televisions off.

2 **Read and match.** 1 – d

1 Turn off the computer when …
2 Don't always use the car – catch …
3 When you brush your teeth, …
4 Take bags with you …
5 Turn off the light …
6 When you live near your school, …

a … you can walk there.
b … turn off the water.
c … when you leave the room.
d … you aren't using it.
e … when you go shopping.
f … a bus or ride a bike.

3 **Think and discuss. What can you do to help the world?**

I walk or ride my bike to school.

Grammar reference

The doll is next to the ball.
The book is on the floor.
The bike is in front of the table.
The helicopter is under the table.
The game is between the doll and the camera.
The kite is behind the bike.

What are you doing?	I'm riding my bike.
What's Daisy doing?	She's reading.
What's Peter doing?	He's flying a kite.
What are Paul and Jane doing?	They're playing hockey.

Is Pete flying a kite?	Yes, he is.
	No, he isn't.

Who's Scott?	He's Sally's brother.
Who's Suzy?	She's Sally's sister.
Who are Grandma and Grandpa Star?	They're Sally's grandparents.

I	like / love / enjoy / don't like/love/enjoy	riding my bike.
He/She	likes / loves / enjoys / doesn't like/love/enjoy	reading about science.
I	want	to ride my bike.
He/She	wants	to read about science.

Do you like taking pictures?	Yes, I do.
Do you want to take a picture?	No, I don't.
Does he/she enjoy playing soccer?	Yes, he/she does.
Does he/she want to play soccer?	No, he/she doesn't.

Does your house have a basement?	My house doesn't have a basement.
	My house has three bedrooms.

What do you do before school? What does he/she do before school?	I have breakfast. He/She has breakfast.
How often do you play in the park? How often does he/she play in the park?	I never / sometimes / always play in the park. I play in the park every day. He/She never / sometimes / always plays in the park. He/She plays in the park every day.

Where do you go to play basketball?	You go to the sports center to play basketball.
Do I have to go to school? Does Scott/Sally have to go to school?	Yes, you do. Yes, he/she does.

What's the matter?	I have / You have / He has / She has / We have / They have a headache. My head hurts.

He has to stay in bed. He shouldn't go to the park.
We have to be quiet in the library. We shouldn't eat in the library.

I'm hungry. I'm cold.	Should I make breakfast? Should I close the window?

weak → weaker thin → thinner naughty → naughtier good → better bad → worse	Parrots are weaker than bears. Dolphins are thinner than whales. Monkeys are naughtier than lions. Sharks are better at swimming than elephants. Pandas are worse at jumping than kangaroos.

What's the weather like?		It's sunny.
I / He / She / It You / We / They	was / wasn't were / weren't	at the park yesterday. at the beach yesterday.
Where were you / they on Saturday? Where was he / she / it on Sunday?		
It There There	was / wasn't was / wasn't were / weren't	cold and windy yesterday. a lot of snow yesterday. a lot of children yesterday.

Movers Listening

1 🎧 93 **Describe the pictures. Listen. Circle the correct picture. There is one example.**

2 🎧 94 😀 **Listen and draw lines. There is one example.**

Clare   Jack   Jim   Fred

Charlie   Sally   Julia

Movers Listening

1 🎧 95 **Listen. Draw the missing information. There is one example.**

2 🎧 96 🐵 **Listen and mark (✓) the box. There is one example.**

Example

What is the story about?

A ✓ B ☐ C ☐

1 What is the matter with Clare today?

A ☐ B ☐ C ☐

2 What is Zoe's brother doing?

A ☐ B ☐ C ☐

3 Who is Paul's science teacher?

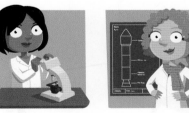 

A ☐ B ☐ C ☐

4 Where were Charlie's socks?

 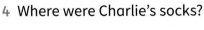

A ☐ B ☐ C ☐

5 What time does Jane have to get up?

A ☐ B ☐ C ☐

Movers Listening

1 Color each thing a different color. Talk to your partner. What's different? Mark (✓).

blanket ☐   towel ☐   flower ☐   one bird ☐   one cloud ☐   sandwich ☐

2 🎧 97 Listen and color and write. There is one example.

Movers Reading and Writing

1 Read. Cross out the word. There is one example.

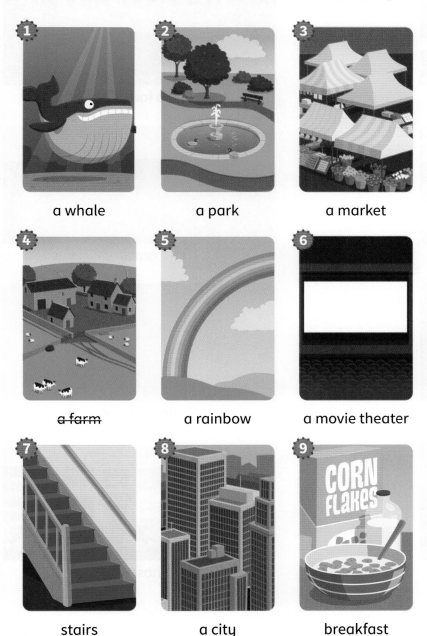

1. a whale
2. a park
3. a market
4. a farm
5. a rainbow
6. a movie theater
7. stairs
8. a city
9. breakfast

Example
Chickens often live here.
_____a farm_____

Questions
1 You go up and down these
when you're inside a house.
_____

2 People can go here to buy food.
_____

3 You sometimes see this
when it's rainy *and* sunny.
_____

4 It's a busy place with a lot
of people, buses, and cars.
_____

5 People go here to see a movie.
_____

6 Children play and have fun here.
_____

2 Write a definition for the two missing words.

(_____) _____

(_____) _____

3 🐵 **Look and read. Choose the correct words and write them on the lines. There is one example.**

a station

a forest

a basement

grass

the country

an elevator

a roof

a hospital

Example

This is a quiet place to live outside the city.   the country

Questions

1 People often go here when they aren't feeling well.

2 This is on top of your house to keep it warm and dry.

3 People wait here to catch a train.

4 This machine takes you up and down a tall building.

5 This grows in fields, and sheep love to eat it.

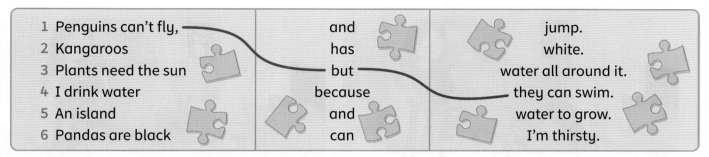

Movers Reading and Writing

1 Read and match. Draw the lines. There is one example.

1 Penguins can't fly,	and	jump.
2 Kangaroos	has	white.
3 Plants need the sun	but	water all around it.
4 I drink water	because	they can swim.
5 An island	and	water to grow.
6 Pandas are black	can	I'm thirsty.

2  **Read the text. Choose the right words and write them on the lines. There is one example.**

Kangaroos

It isn't easy to see kangaroos (example) ___because___ they only live in a country called Australia. They eat grass, but they don't need (1) _____ water.

Kangaroos are different from other animals because they cannot run or walk. They (2) _____. They (3) _____ one of the few animals in the world that move around in this way.

Their two strong legs, huge feet, and long tail help them jump. They can also (4) _____ very well.

Did you know that when kangaroos stand up, they are (5) _____ than a person?

Example: then (because) but

1	many	a	a lot of
2	hop	hops	hopping
3	is	are	was
4	swim	swam	swimming
5	tall	taller	more tall

Movers Speaking

1 **Look. Find the differences. Complete the sentences. There is one example.**

Example: The bed is pink in this picture, but in this one it's _____orange_____ .

1 In this picture the girl has brown hair, but here she has _____ hair.
2 The jacket is red, but this one's _____ .
3 Here you can see a dolphin, but here there's a _____ .
4 There's a cabinet behind the door, but here there's a _____ .
5 Here the girl is holding a book, but here she has a _____ .

2 **Look. Find the differences. Talk about the pictures.**

Movers Speaking

1 **Look. Tell the story with your partner. Read and number. There is one example.**

A dolphin helps

Example: The girl is crying. `3`

The family is driving to the beach. ☐   The girl is sitting on her dad's shoulders. ☐

A dolphin has the ball. ☐   The boy can't get the ball. ☐

The children are playing with a ball. ☐   Dad is taking a picture. ☐

Mom is eating a sandwich. ☐   The family is watching the dolphin. ☐

2 🎧 98 😊 **Look and listen. Then continue the story.**

Picnic time by the river

Thanks and Acknowledgements

Authors' thanks

The authors and publishers acknowledgements the following sources of copyright material and are grateful for the permissions granted. While every effort has been made, it has not always been possible to identify the sources of all the material used or to trace all copyright holders. If any omissions are brought to our notice, we will be happy to include the appropriate acknowledgments on reprinting and in the next update to the digital edition, as applicable.

Key: U = Unit, R = Review, V= Values

General

Many thanks to everyone at Cambridge University Press & Assessment for their dedication and hard work, and in particular to: Liane Grainger and Lynn Townsend for supervising the whole project and guiding us calmly through the storms; Zara Hutchinson-Goncalves for her energy, enthusiasm, and expertise. Thanks for doing such a great job.

We would also like to thank all our students and colleagues, past, present, and future, at Star English academy in Murcia, especially Jim Kelly for his friendship and support throughout the years.

For the women who were my pillars of strength when I most needed it: Milagros Marin, Sara de Alba, Elia Navarro, and Maricarmen Balsalobre. – CN

To Pablo and Carlota. This one's for you. *Kid's Box*'s biggest fans. – MT

Photography

All the photos are sourced from Getty Images.

U0: chuckcollier/E+; **U1:** Morsa Images/E+; Ariel Skelley/DigitalVision; JGI/Jamie Grill; **U2:** Rosemary Calvert/Photodisc; Nazar Abbas Photography/Moment; Daniel Bosma/Moment; Canetti/iStock/Getty Images Plus; alabn/iStock/Getty Images Plus; Julien McRoberts/VectorPocket/iStock/Getty Images Plus; Francesco Riccardo Iacomino/Moment; photography by Sanchai Loongroong/Moment; ManuelVelasco/E+; Alex Levine/500px; Sydney James/DigitalVision; bombuscreative/DigitalVision Vectors; Cavan Images; **U3:** DigiPub/Moment; Jieophoto/iStock/Getty Images Plus; Wa Nity Canthra/EyeEm; Irina Cheremisinova/iStock/Getty Images Plus; Pakhnyushchyy/iStock/Getty Images Plus; asikkk/iStock/Getty Images Plus; Kyryl Gorlov/iStock/Getty Images Plus; Ninel Roshchina/iStock/Getty Images Plus; Lumi Images/Sveinn Baldvinsson; Jonathan Knowles/Stone; Matthias Kulka/The Image Bank; Jonathan Knowles/Stone RF; **U4:** d3sign/Moment; Iryna Veklich/Moment; RichVintage/E+; Colors Hunter – Chasseur de Couleurs/Moment Open; M_a_y_a/E+; D. Sharon Pruitt Pink Sherbet Photography/Moment; Karen M. Romanko/Photodisc; Kei Uesugi/Stone; RBB/Moment; joSon/Stone; **U5:** Yoshiyoshi Hirokawa/DigitalVision; Tom Le Goff/Photodisc; stefanamer/iStock/Getty Images Plus; parinyabinsuk/iStock/Getty Images Plus; Weerameth Weerachotewong/EyeEm ; AaronAmat/iStock/Getty Images Plus; sdominick/iStock/Getty Images Plus; Photodjo/iStock/Getty Images Plus; yourstockbank/iStock/Getty Images Plus; LittleBee80/iStock/Getty Images Plus; vitapix/iStock/Getty Images Plus; Khosrork/iStock/Getty Images Plus; Suriya Silsaksom/EyeEm; Virojt Changyencham/Moment; Mint Images/Mint Images RF; clubfoto/iStock/Getty Images Plus; alkir/iStock/Getty Images Plus; SCIENCE PHOTO LIBRARY/Science Photo Library; Kiyoshi Hijiki/Moment; Jena Ardell/Moment; kuritafsheen/RooM; Anjelika Gretskaia/Moment; paci77/DigitalVision Vectors; LPETTET/DigitalVision Vectors; MIXA; Iryna Veklich/Moment; Burke/Triolo Productions/The Image Bank; BSIP; vitapix/E+; Jose Luis Pelaez Inc/DigitalVision; Kwanchai Chai-Udom/EyeEm; Science Photo Library; Rob Lewine; Raimund Koch/The Image Bank; fcafotodigital/E+; **U6:** Mint Images/Mint Images RF; yongyuan/E+; Images By Tang Ming Tung/Stone; JohnnyGreig/E+; gahsoon/E+; **U7:** IronHeart/Moment; Mike Hill/Stone; Simon McGill/Moment; Nimit Virdi/500px; Glowimages; Image Source; Lazareva/iStock/Getty Images Plus; Rüdiger Katterwe/EyeEm; USO/iStock/Getty Images Plus; Raimund Linke/The Image Bank; Gerard Soury/The Image Bank; JAH/iStock/Getty Images Plus; Fotosearch; SKapl/iStock/Getty Images Plus; SunRay BRI Cattery RU/iStock/Getty Images Plus; Nerthuz/iStock/Getty Images Plus; texcroc/E+; Hung_Chung_Chih/iStock/Getty Images Plus; goldhafen/E+; spxChrome/E+; Jonathan Fromager/EyeEm; Freder/E+; Martin Harvey/DigitalVision; amar pixler/500px Prime; Savushkin/E+; Claude LeTien/Moment; milehightraveler/E+; Steven Greenfield/500px; Trey Thomas/500px Prime; Glowimages; Stuart Westmorland/Corbis Documentary; jez_bennett/iStock/Getty Images Plus; **U8:** Marco Bottigelli/Moment; Danica Jovanov/iStock/Getty Images Plus; spanteldotru/E+; Bobbushphoto/iStock/Getty Images Plus; Os Tartarouchos/Moment; Peter Zelei Images/Moment; standret/iStock/Getty Images Plus; Thanapol Kuptanisakorn/EyeEm; Westend61; Moof/Image Source; George Doyle/Stockbyte; Andrea Evangelo-Giamou/EyeEm; ManoAfrica/E+; Trịnh Ngọc Đại/500Px Plus; Paul Souders/Stone; Rodrigo Echevarria/EyeEm; Pablo Perdomo/Moment; Peter Yates/500px; lindsay_imagery/E+; Lelia Valduga/Moment; gradyreese/E+; Berit Myrekrok/Photodisc; **R12:** Oscar Martín/Moment; Image Source; Michael Blann/Stone; studiocasper/E+; JGI/Tom Grill; fotoVoyager/iStock/Getty Images Plus; Working In Media/iStock/Getty Images Plus; allanswart/iStock/Getty Images Plus; alabn/iStock/Getty Images Plus; John Lawson, Belhaven/Moment Open; Westend61; Kevin Brine/iStock/Getty Images Plus; Simon McGill/Moment; scibak/E+; Pgiam/iStock/Getty Images Plus; Thomas M. Scheer/EyeEm; Emma Kim/Image Source; Image Source/Steve Prezant; Nastia11/iStock/Getty Images Plus; Morsa Images/DigitalVision; Roy Cheung/500px Prime; imaginima/iStock/Getty Images Plus; John Keeble/Moment; Nikola Ilic/E+; Maskot; monkeybusinessimages/iStock/Getty Images Plus; manley099/E+; DonNichols/E+; Wa Nity Canthra/EyeEm; Chiradech/iStock/Getty Images Plus; tiler84/iStock/Getty Images Plus; ManuelVelasco/E+; Sydney James/DigitalVision; **R34:** swetta/E+; baona/E+; Csondy/E+; shilh/iStock/Getty Images Plus; Barry Winiker/Photodisc; Glasshouse Images/The Image Bank Unreleased; Brian Keith Lorraine/Moment; photography by p. lubas/Moment; **R78:** Freder/iStock/Getty Images Plus; kertlis/E+; Colin Horn/Moment; sizsus/iStock/Getty Images Plus; GlobalP/iStock/Getty Images Plus; SEAN GLADWELL/Moment; anderm/iStock/Getty Images Plus; JulyKat/iStock/Getty Images Plus; apple2499/iStock/Getty Images Plus; mikroman6/Moment; Chris McLoughlin/Moment; KEHAN CHEN/Moment; Image Source; borchee/E+; Vivien.x.Li/Moment; swetta/E+; AlesVeluscek/E+; Daniel Rogers-Bromley/EyeEm; sebastian-julian/iStock/Getty Images Plus; GK Hart/Vikki Hart/DigitalVision; TanyaRozhnovskaya/iStock/Getty Images Plus; hadynyah/E+; Peter Gabriels/EyeEm; NYS444/iStock/Getty Images Plus; Photos by R A Kearton/Moment; WAS_/iStock/Getty Images Plus; shilh/iStock/Getty Images Plus; **V12:** Jakovo/iStock/Getty Images Plus; fstop123/E+; SolStock/E+; Hill Street Studios/DigitalVision; fanjianhua/Moment; **V34:** nature/iStock/Getty Images Plus; Patricia Marroquin/Moment; simon2579/DigitalVision Vectors; Carmen Martínez Torrón/Moment; **V56:** Comstock/Stockbyte; Productions/E+; Syldavia/iStock/Getty Images Plus; Lorado/E+; **V78:** Sasi Ponchaisang/EyeEm; Ronnie Kaufman/DigitalVision; SDI Productions/E+; lolostock/iStock/Getty Images Plus.

Illustrations

Antonio Cuesta (direct); Marek Jagucki (direct); Carol Herring, Leo Trinidad (Bright); Michael McCabe, Diego Diaz, Gustavo Berardo, Ilias Arahovitis (Beehive); Pronk Media Inc.

Cover illustration by Pronk Media Inc.

Audio

Audio managed by Hyphen Publishing, produced by New York Audio Productions and John Marshall Media

Songs composed by Robert Lee

Video

Video acknowledgments are in the Teacher Resources on Cambridge One.

Design and typeset

Blooberry Design

Additional authors

Katy Kelly: Lock's Sounds and spelling
Rebecca Legros: math, geography, science, and music sections
Montse Watkin: Exam Folders

Freelance editor

Wendy Cherry